In a Cave

by Jennifer Boothroyd

first step nonfiction

Lerner Publications Company · Minneapolis

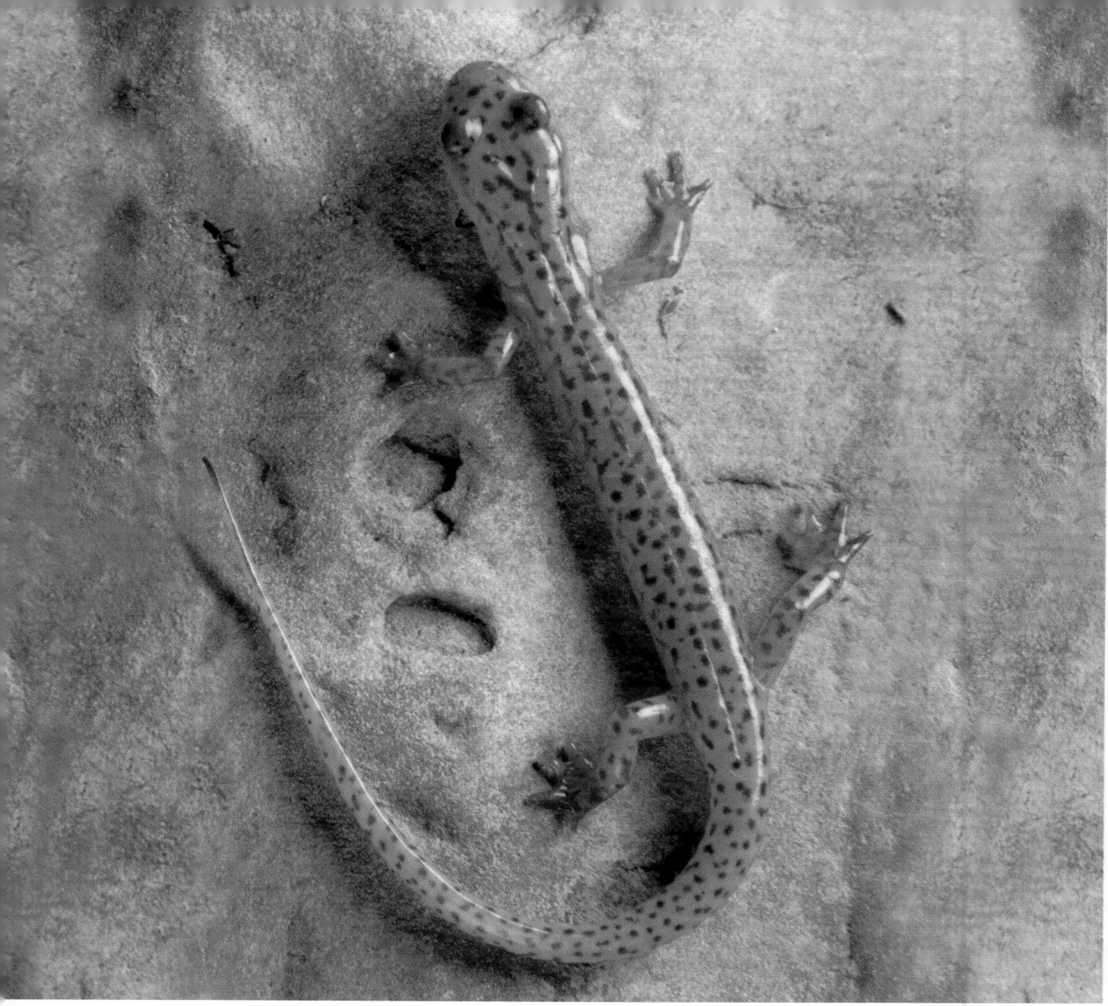

What lives in a cave?

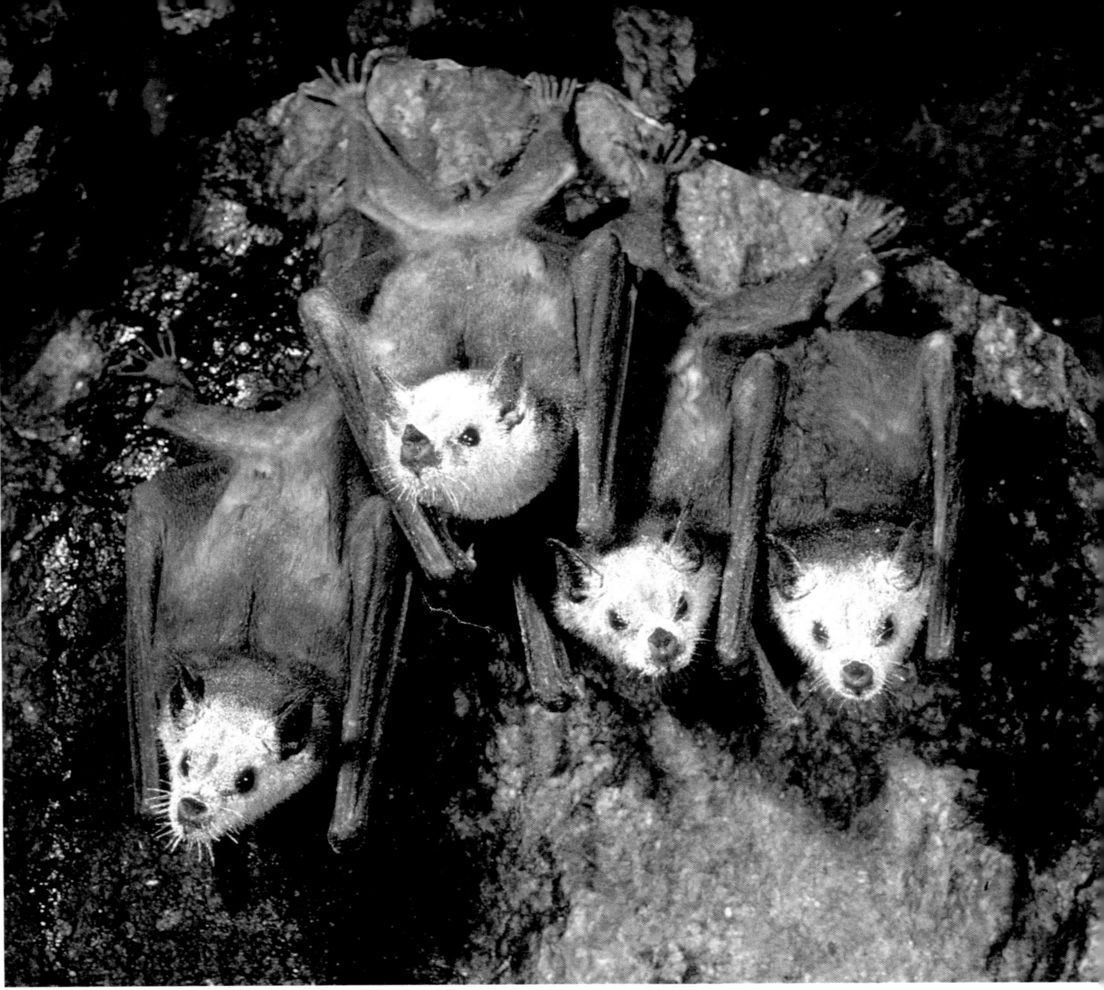

Bats

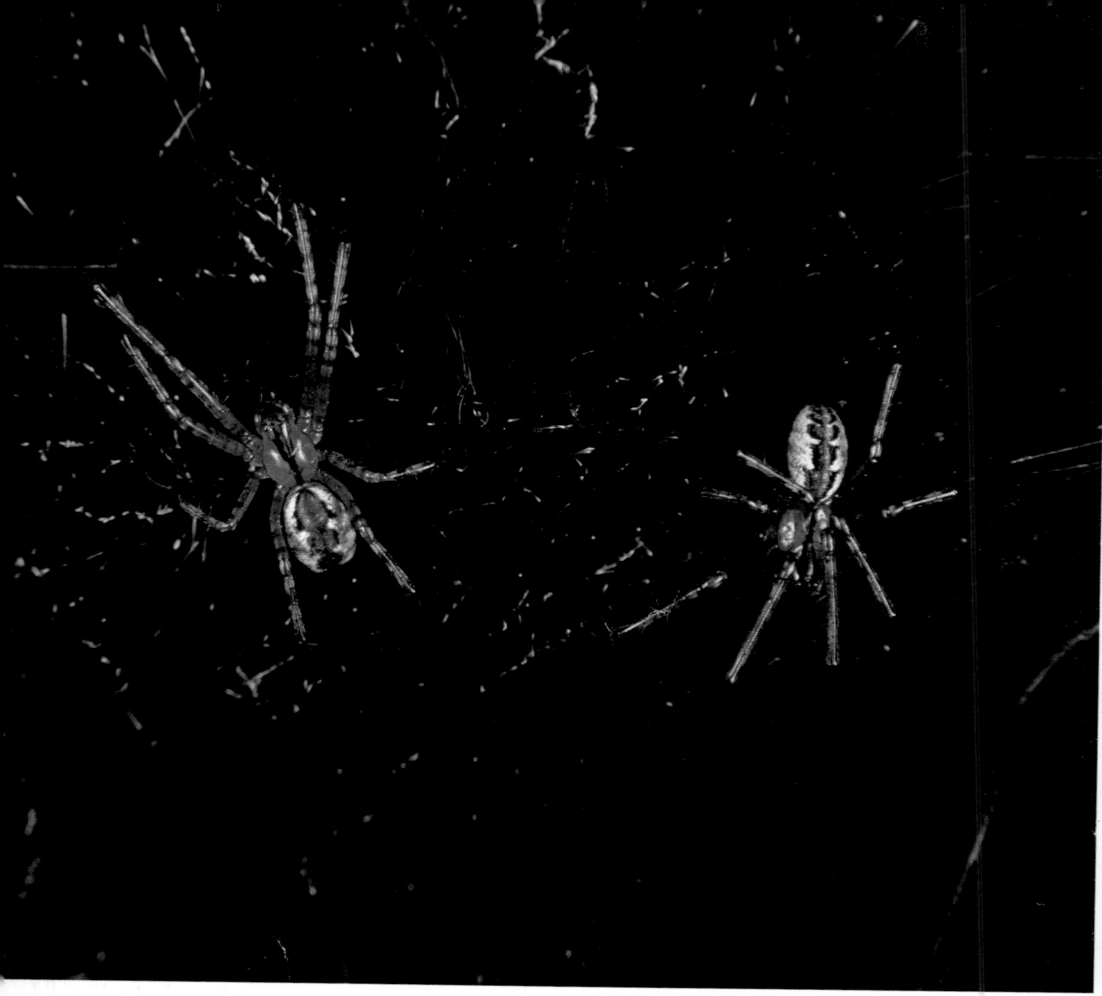

Spiders

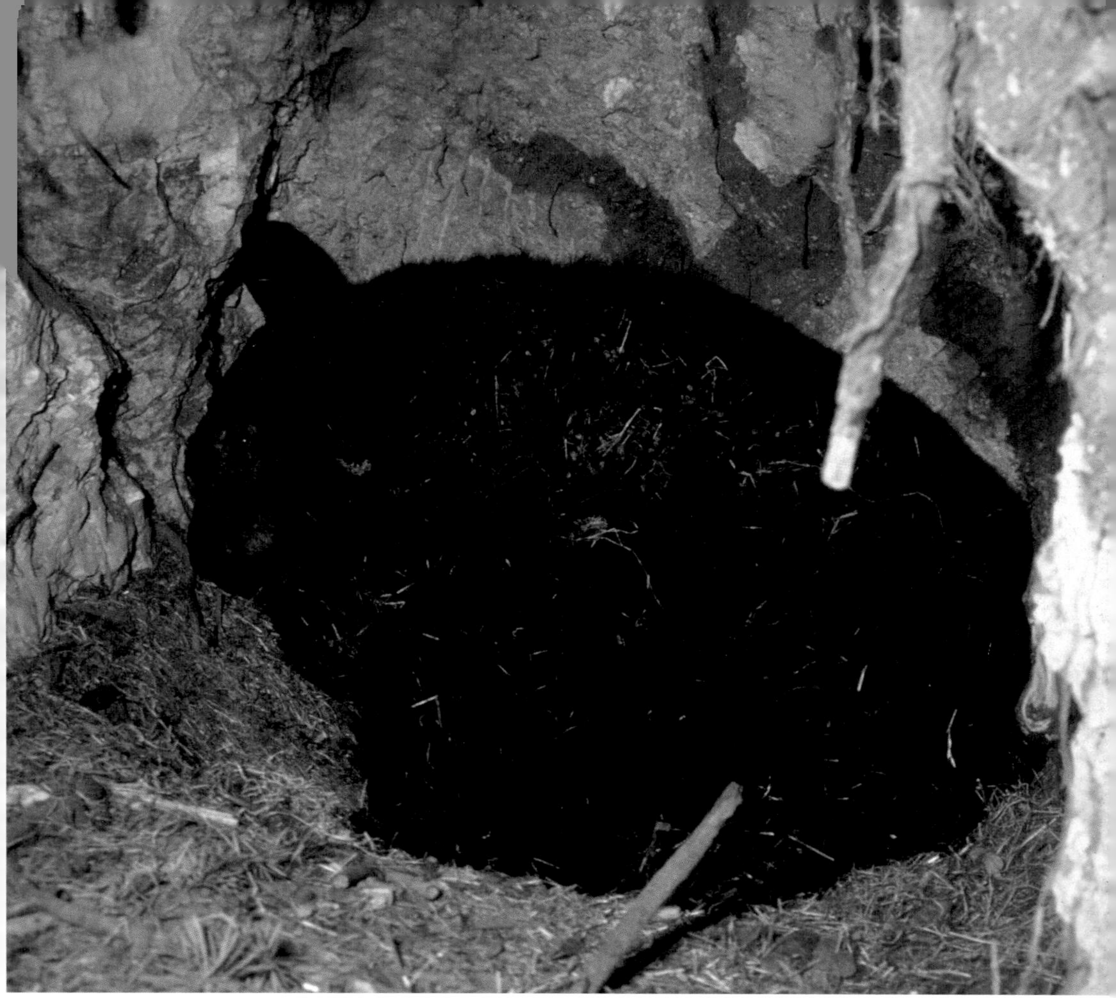

Bears

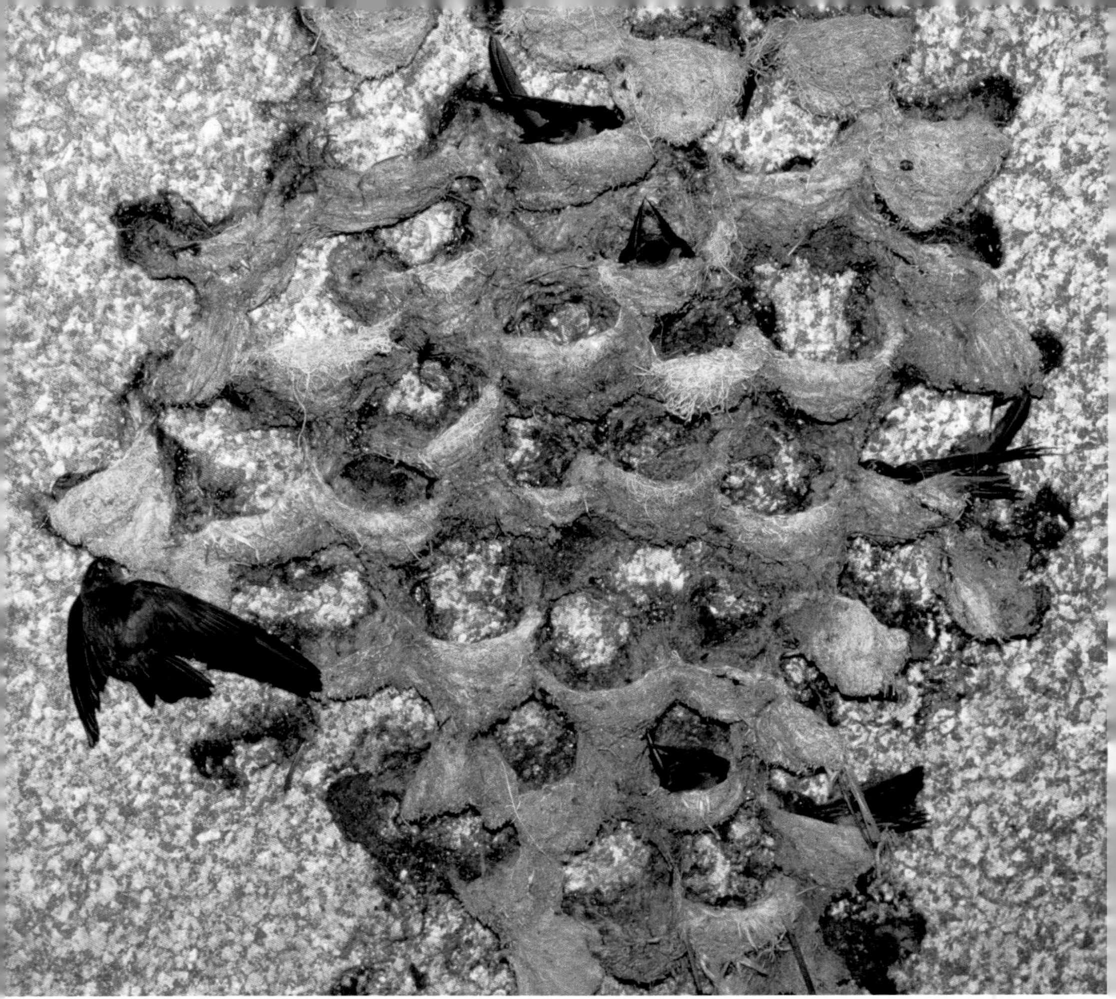

Birds

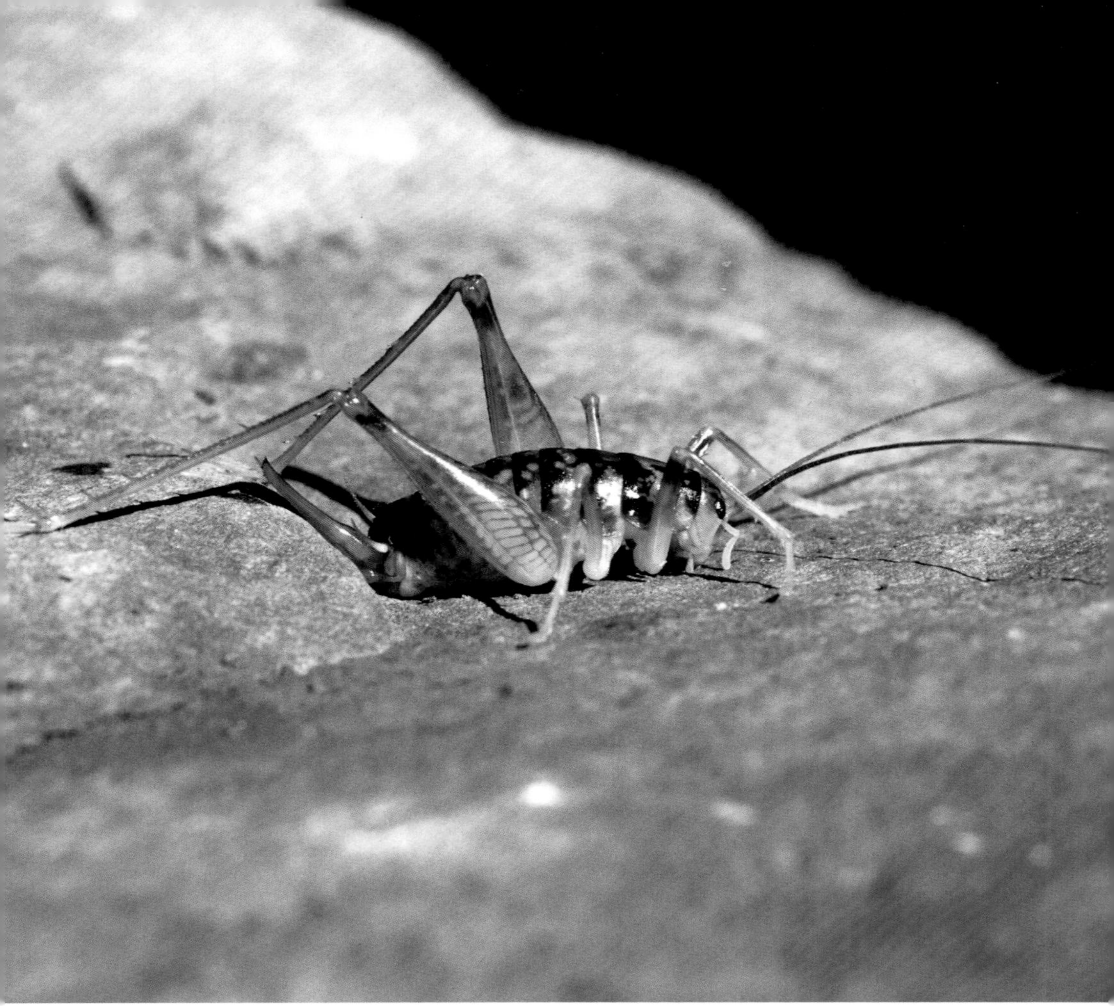

Crickets

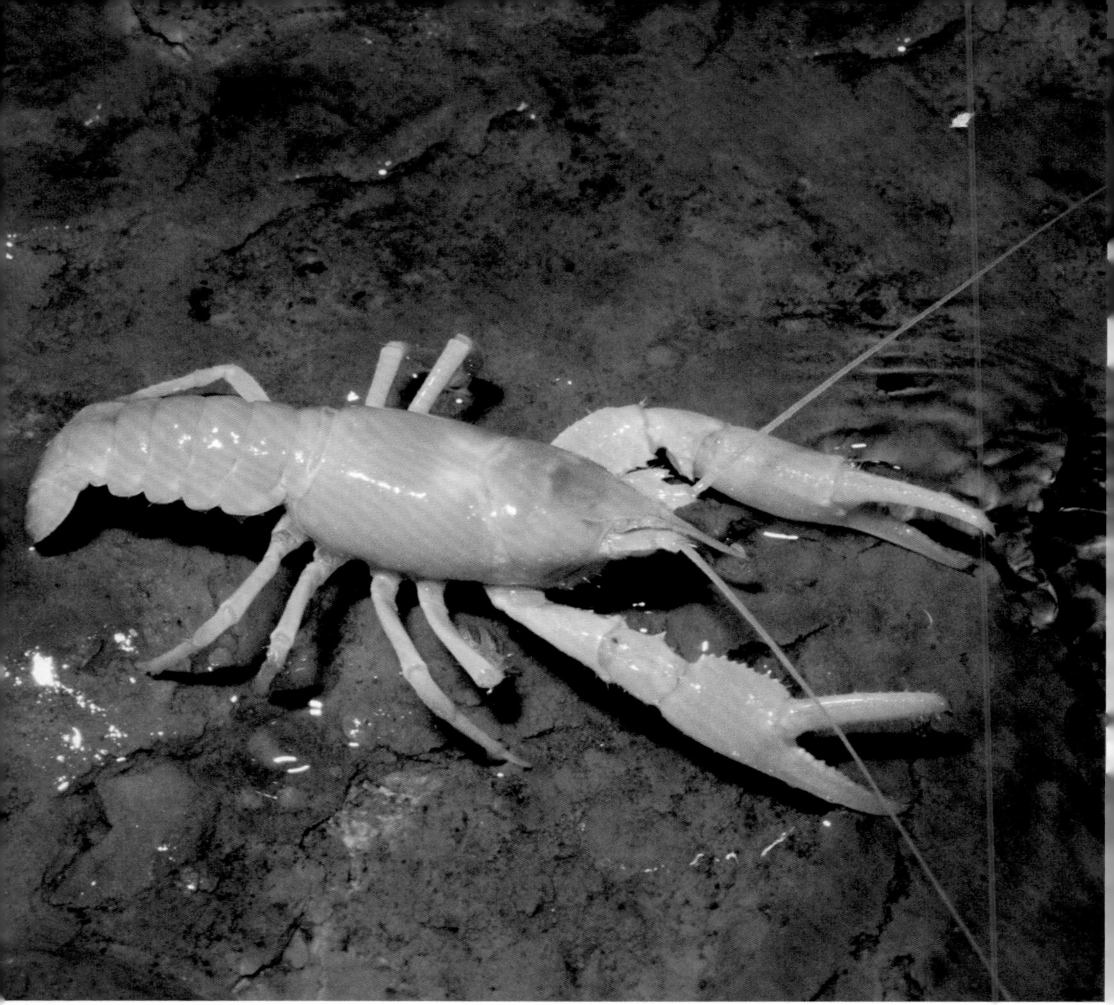

Crayfish